It is Important to Become...

Written By: Ty Ron Stidam
Illustrated by Bobooks

Copyright © 2022 by Ty Ron Stidam
All Rights Reserved.
No part of this book may be reproduced, distributed, or transmitted in any form or by any means, including photocopying, recording, or other electronic or mechanical methods, without the prior written consent of the copyright owner, except in the case of brief quotation embodied in critical articles, reviews, and certain other noncommercial uses permitted by copyright law.

I decided to write this book because I felt it was important for black kids to understand that they will encounter more obstacles in life than the average person. Throughout American history and even the present day, wrongdoings against black people have remained constant. Disparities toward black people have never ended and are cyclic as they shift from one form to another. There is always a false sense of subsiding and then resurging again even though in truth the mistreatment remains. I think children must realize that most of the same discriminative people, laws and the justice system from the past are still relevant today. Now so more than ever we need to do a better job of relaying the message to our children. I hope to encourage and ignite a fire of great purpose in them to become the change that we need.

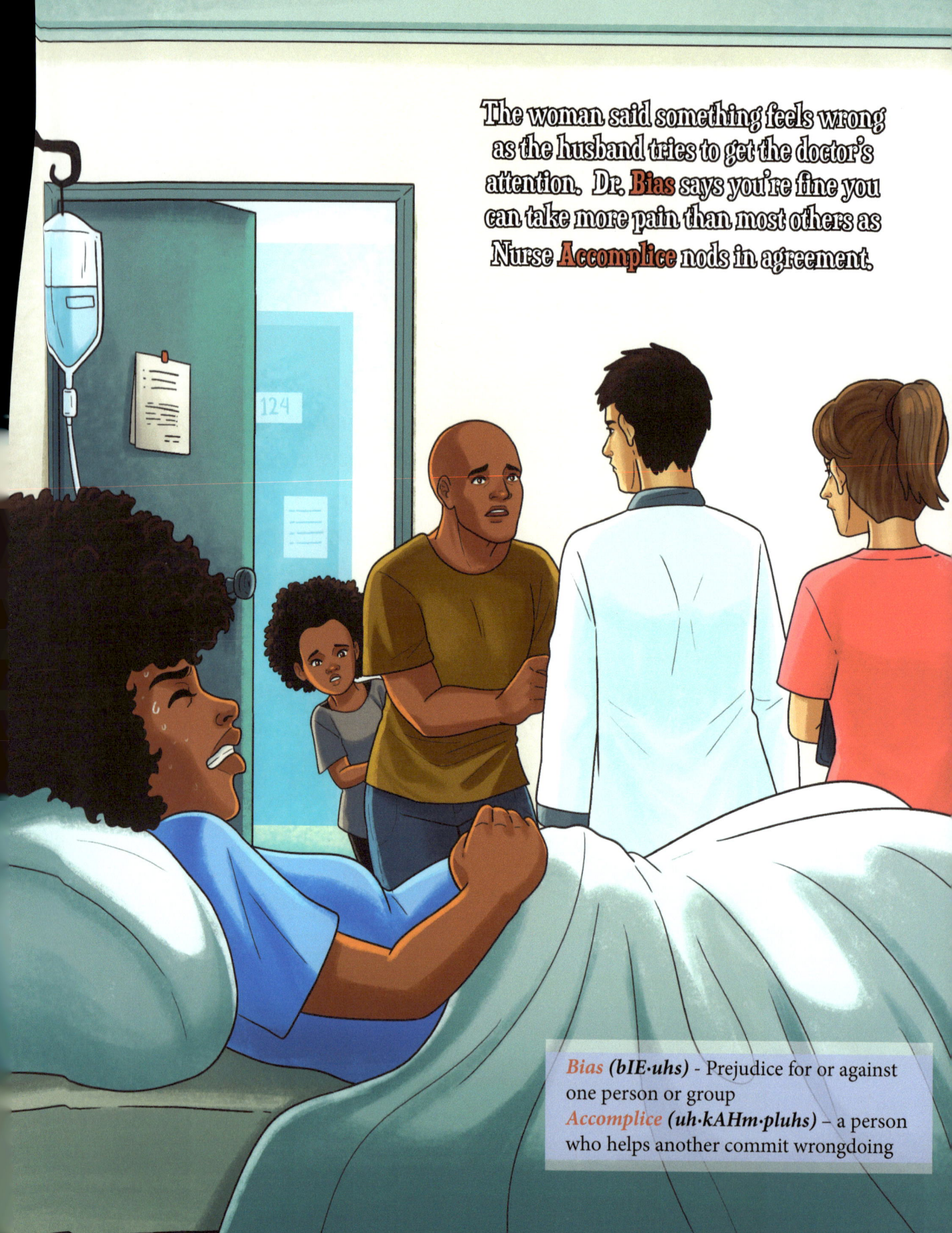

Something feels wrong, explains the woman to the doctor as the husband urgently gets the doctor's attention. Dr. Ebony checks out the woman and assures her that scans will be run before and after delivery to ensure that everything is okay.

Dr. Ebony, "It was a matter of life and death for me to become a doctor to ensure that all patients get the same treatment no matter how they look."

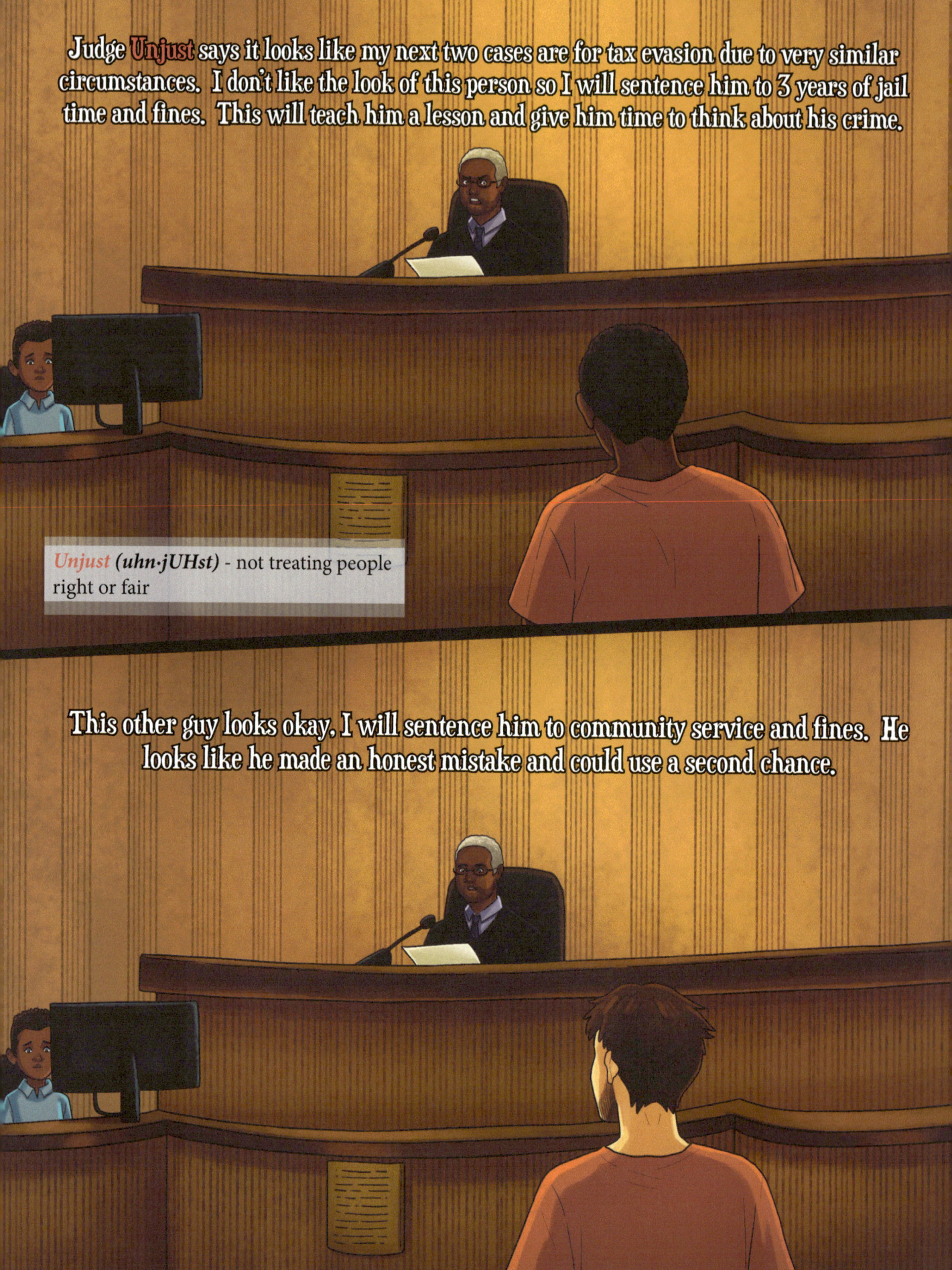

Team Balanced handed out large checks that fully funded all scientific groups' research that would make the most difference in the world.

Team Balanced "It was meaningful that we work in philanthropy to ensure that all groups get a fair share of funding to make sure research includes not some but all people."

Meaningful (mEE·ning·fuhl) – full of purpose or value

Mr. Rigged worked on an algorithm that made his social media platform limit the number of followers that would see postings from certain users.

Rigged (rIgd) - Having an outcome dishonestly predetermined

Mr. Daniel worked on an algorithm that would be fair to all users by not imposing limitations and letting all followers see all posted content by their favorite social media users.

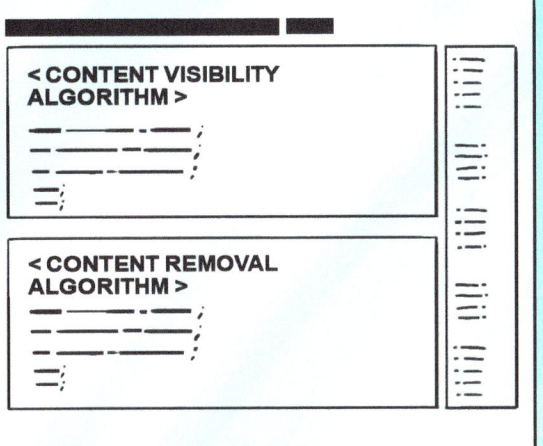

Daniel "It is a huge benefit that I became a programmer to make sure our challenges in life did not become our challenges online."

Zaria's Home Services provided the family with a fair offer for the work to be done and the family agreed.

Ms. Zaria "It was **consequential** for me to help families fulfill their service needs. Otherwise, many families would not be able to afford services and homes & communities would be in disrepair."

Consequential (kahn·suh·kwEn·shuhl)
- having important effects or results

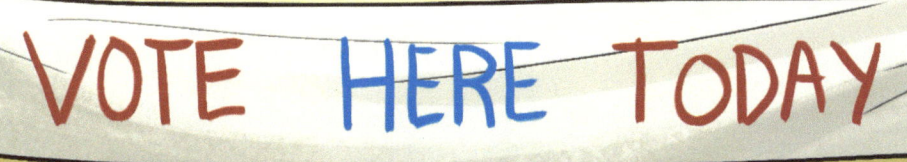
VOTE HERE TODAY

Mr. Amir turned into the first polling place he saw as he was eager to make sure his voice was heard and his vote was counted.

Mr. Amir "I must vote as often as possible because it's the only way for things to change."

YOUR VOTE DOES NOT MATTER KEEP DRIVING

Mrs. **Misguide** showed up-and-coming neighborhoods to certain families while promoting unfavorable homes and broken neighborhoods to others.

Misguide (*mis·gIEd*) - To tell an untruth or falsehood

Ms. Shayla showed up-and-coming neighborhoods and homes to all families which would be a great return on investment in the future.

Ms. Shayla "I want great neighborhoods and homes to be available to all people."

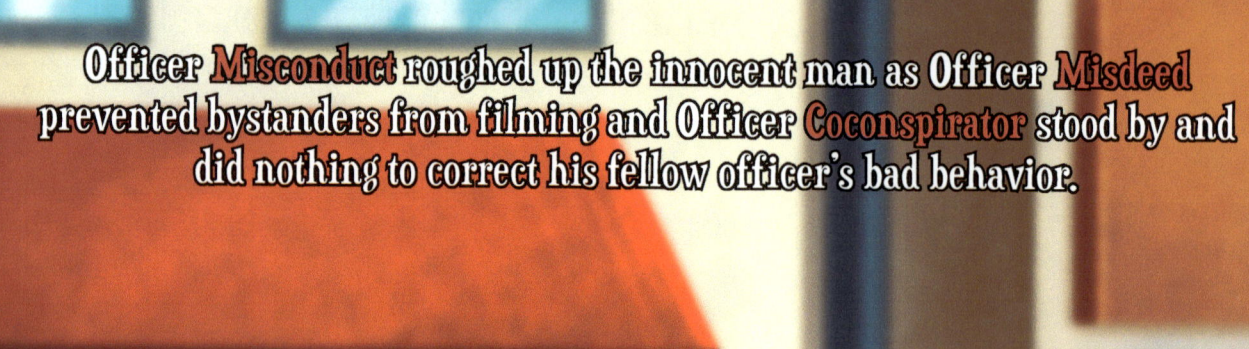

Officer Misconduct roughed up the innocent man as Officer Misdeed prevented bystanders from filming and Officer Coconspirator stood by and did nothing to correct his fellow officer's bad behavior.

Misconduct (mis·kAHn·duhkt) - an act of wrongdoing or improper behavior

Misdeed (mis·di·d) - act or judgment that is wrong

Coconspirator (kOH·kuhn·spIR·uh·tuhr) - A person who helps another commit a crime or wrongdoing

Sergeant Shaniyah prevented Officer Misconduct from doing any bad behavior that wasn't appropriate according to the law.
Sergeant Shaniyah "It was dire that I became a police officer to make sure that we as police follow a higher standard than what we expect from others."

Dire (dIE·uhr) - Urgent; desperate

Ms. **Premeditated** decided that during record low-interest rates at her bank she would deny certain customers regardless of whether they qualified and approve others who did not qualify.

RECORD LOW INTEREST
2.75%

Credit score 800 & Credit Score 820
Current Interest Rate: 5.75%
Equity of home $100K
Debt-To-Income Ratio: 17% & 25%
Auto Status: Approve
Override Status: Denied

Premeditated (pree·mEd·uh·tay·tuhd) - planned; carefully weighed or considered

Ms. Layla Sky reported both City University & State University students got a little out of hand after a championship win.
Ms. Layla "It was key for me to become a reporter and make sure all stories are reported truthfully and equally."

These are just a few reasons why you need to become.

The End

The timeline that you are about to view is but a small sampling. The dates provided on the charts are rough estimates based on actual historical events. Summarizations of historical events do not capture the great depth and impact of how these events affect everyday life. It is recommended that you research each event separately to have a better understanding of what exactly unfolded during that historical moment.

MISTREATMENT
of Black People in America

  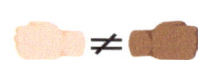

1518 - 1860
Transatlantic Slave Trade (Inhumane Voyage)
Kidnapped slaves (hostages) were brought across the seas in inhumane conditions that often killed half of the slaves (hostages) before reaching their destination.

1619 - 1865
Slavery (Human Trafficking)
After the tobacco worker strike human traffickers began to use hostages in Jamestown Virginia (Colony established 1607)

1619 - Present
Colorism
The practice of enslaving Africans based on skin color; in addition to the divide and conquer strategy of treating black people with lighter skin tones more favorable than those of darker tones. Effects of which remain global today.

1775 - 1783
States Rights
The argument that state law can supersede federal or national law mostly pertains to maintaining slavery against federal regulation.

1714 - 1964
Sundown Towns
Community of all white people which requires black people to either be out by sundown or not visit at all.

1705 - 1865
Slave Codes
Stripped all black people free or indentured of rights to control them.

1619 - Present
Massacres
Mass killings of black people either due to hate, jealousy or to put an end to economic success (wealth) black communities had achieved.

1787 - 1787
Fugitive Slave Clause
Preventing escaped slaves from claiming freedom when escaping to a free state gave enslavers the right to claim slaves.

1789 - 1789
Three-fifths Compromise
3/5 of the total number of black people = to one person (Northern abolitionists' way of limiting southern representation in Congress).

1808 - 1808
Importation Ban
Congress bans the importation of slaves (hostages).

1820 - 1839
Black Literacy Ban
Prevented black people from learning how to read or write.

1846 - 1933
Convict Leasing
Government leasing of inmates to keep the southern economy moving with a nearly free labor force. Leased to railways, mines, and plantations and were subject to inhumane conditions.

1845 - 1865
Manifest Destiny
A belief to force natives off the land and expand slavery to build the nation.

1829 - Present
Race Riots
Riots that occur over racial tensions between black and white people. Oftentimes results in the loss of life of black people.

1820 - 1857
Missouri Compromise
Allowed union statehood while maintaining a balance between slave states and free states.

1850 - 1850
Industrial Slavery
Bibb Steam Mill Company Corporations began owning slaves in addition to rich plantation owners.

1850 - 1861
Fugitive Slave Act
Forced abolitionists to turn in escaped slaves or be prosecuted to extent of the law.

1857 - 1857
Dred Scott Supreme Court Decision
Black people had no rights, were considered inferior, and were not included as citizens mentioned in the constitution.

1859 - 1945
Eugenics
Ideal to keep white people dominant through genetics as a way to advance the population.

1861 - 1861
Confiscation act of 1861
Northern act of classifying escaped southern slaves as contraband of war; still viewed slaves as property, not people.

1861 - 1861
Sequestration Act of 1861
Factories owned by Northerners were confiscated by southerners and utilized slave labor.

1861 - 1865
Southern Secession
In order to preserve slavery southern states succeed from the union.

1861 - 1861
Cornerstone speech
Alexander H. Stevens VP of the Confederacy stated that black people should be subservient to white people in the new government and confederate states will succeed from the Union because of it.

Soldier

continue...

1861 - 1865
Civil War
American war over slavery.

1861 - 1862
Abraham Lincoln's Letter to Horace Greeley
President admits that his goal was solely to keep the union together whatever result of slavery he chooses would have to be the best option for the union.

1863 - 1863
Emancipation Proclamation
Allowed the Union army to enlist black men to fight in the war in an effort to change the way black people were viewed.

1863 - 1865
Confederate Government
Purchased Briar Field Ironworks in Alabama utilized slave labor (black men listed as livestock).

1865 - 1865
Special Field Order 15
Divided up 400 thousand acres amongst freedmen with 40 acres and a mule to each family.

1865 - 1865
Freedman Bureau
Protect the rights of freed slaves and assist with the distribution of 40 acres of land.

1865 - 1865
Lincoln Assassination
President Lincoln was killed resulting in known racist becoming president.

1865 - 1964
Labor Contracts
Black people were forced into slave conditions through contracts.

1865 - 1877
Reconstruction
Federal Troops protected rights for newly freed slaves allowing black males equality and voting rights.

1865 - 1872
KKK
American terrorist organization.

1865 - 1869
Andrew Johnson new President
The belief of country & government for white men only (Letter to Missouri Governor 1866).

  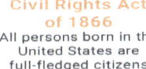

1865 - 1964
Segregation
The systematic separation of people into racial or other ethnic groups in daily life.

1866 - 1866
Freedman Bureau
By order of President Andrew Johnson made freedmen (black people) return the land over to white ownership.

1866 - 1866
Civil Rights Act of 1866
All persons born in the United States are full-fledged citizens (Andrew Johnson vetoed congress override).

1867 - 1867
Reconstruction Act of 1867
Contained conditions for confederate states to comply with before joining back into the union. (Andrew Johnson's veto was overridden by Congress)

1877 - 1877
Compromise of 1877
Southern Democrats under President Rutherford B. Hayes pulled federal troops from the south. Eliminating protections for newly freed black people and undoing the Reconstruction period.

1870 - 1870
Federal Gov Declaration of KKK
Deemed terrorist organization by federal government disbanded by 1872.

1868 - 1868
14th Amendment
Granted citizenship and equal civil and legal rights to black people and enslaved people who had been emancipated after the American Civil War. (Andrew Johnson denounced and referred to as States' Rights' was overridden by Congress)

1877 - 1941
Neo Slavery (2nd Slavery)
The new form of slavery after chattel slavery was abolished consisted of debt peonage, industrial slavery & convict leasing. Often more cruel practices than plantation slavery because it did not require the preservation of slaves.

1877 - 1941
Debt Peonage
Slavery contract black people had to adhere to until the debt was paid off with labor usually keeping them in debt by false billings of food and lodging.

1877 - 1964
Black Codes
Vagrancy, trespassing, drinking, gambling, riding the train without a ticket, and obscene language were the petty crimes that got black people arrested and sentenced to hard labor.

1877 - Present
Policing
Unfair harassment, arrest, and killings of black people.

1877 - Present
Lynching
The murder of black people without trial or jury.

1877 - Present
Confessing Judgement
Black people falsely accept judgment in order to avoid more harsh sentencing by trial.

1877 - 1964
Pig Laws
Was the process of elevating petty crimes to felonies for black people to force them into industrial slavery.

1883 - 1883
Civil Rights Cases Supreme Court
The Civil Rights Act of 1875 was reversed by the supreme court.

1896 - 1896
Homer Plessy Supreme Court
Federal Approval of Segregation 1/8 black Plessy was arrested in 1892 for failure to remove from the whites-only railcar.

1900 - 2015
Brown paper Bag Test
Due to the effects of colorism, many lighter-toned black people began throwing exclusive events where admittance was based on skin tone being lighter than a brown paper bag.

1901 - 1965
Disenfranchisement
Deprived black people of the right to vote usually through literacy tests, poll taxes, or intimidation. Caused no black jurors or black people to reside in government.

continue...

  **KKK**

1915 - 1915
Birth Of a Nation
Originally called the Clansman a film that depicted black people as unintelligent and immoral.

1915 - 1915
President Woodrow Wilson
Viewed Birth of a Nation film in the White House.

1915 - Present
Rebirth of the KKK
Ku Klux Klan Americas white supremacist, a terrorist hate group.

1932 - 1972
Tuskeegee Experiment
The largest known illegal medical experimentation on black people resulted in purposefully infecting black people with syphilis.

1941 - 1941
Circular 3591
Mandated FBI rebrand cases of peonage to involuntary servitude or slavery and prosecute as crimes.

1936 - 1967
Green Book
Hugo Victor Green created a guidebook for black people that included restaurants, hotels, gas & drug stores that were necessary for safe travel. Black people would otherwise be turned away, humiliated, or harmed for seeking service while traveling within parts of the country.

1933 - 1988
Redlining
Government-sponsored housing segregation plan to curb housing shortage by providing housing to white people while pushing black people to projects. Loans were usually approved for white areas and denied for black and mixed races. Also responsible for creating an even larger wealth gap between black people and whites.

1942 - 1942
Alfred Irving
Last chattel slave known to be freed in America.

1956 - 1971
Cointel Pro
Illegal projects conducted by the United States Federal Bureau of Investigation (FBI) aimed at surveilling, infiltrating, discrediting, and disrupting domestic American political organizations. Primarily black leaders and black organizations were often harassed, infiltrated & dismantled.

1964 - 1964
Civil Rights Act 1964
Prohibits discrimination based on race, color, religion, sex, or national origin

1965 - 1965
Voting Rights Act 1965
Ends discriminatory voting practices (disenfranchisement).

1994 - Present
Three Strike Law
Law that allowed for longer sentencing with multiple offenses. Oftentimes black people would be convicted of multiple petty crimes that under 3 strikes law would allow them to be sentenced longer without a chance of probation.

1971 - Present
War on Drugs
Nixon's policy disenfranchised black people intentionally by imprisonment.

1970 - Present
Mass Incarceration
Disproportionate incarceration of black people.

1994 - Present
Crime Bill 1994
Law proposed by Joe Biden & signed by Bill Clinton incentivized state and local government through federal funding (taxpayer dollars) to build more prisons, arrest more people and enact harsher sentencing that disproportionately affects African Americans.

2017 - 2017
FBI Black Identity Extremist Classification
FBI classifies Black Identity Extremists (BIEs) as the highest terror threat more so than any other group Unwarranted BIE classification was so broad that you can literally classify any African American as BIE.

2020 - 2020
74 Million Americans
74 million people voted for President Trump after evident ties of supporting white nationalism that often coincides with white supremacy.

2022 - Present
Supreme Court Decision
Supreme court guts wrongful conviction lifeline in favor of racist troupe 'States rights' which will largely affect innocent black people from being released from wrongful state convictions.

2021 - Present
Voting Law Restrictions
Republican Governors pass restrictive laws to limit voting for certain groups.

2021 - Present
Restrictions of teaching Black History
Republican Governors pass restrictive laws about teaching black history in schools.

Event	Start Date	End Date	Summary
Transatlantic Slave Trade (Inhumane Voyage)	1518	1860	Kidnapped slaves (hostages) were brought across the seas in inhumane conditions that often killed half of the slaves (hostages) before reaching their destination.
Slavery (Human Trafficking)	1619	1865	After the tobacco worker strike human traffickers began to use hostages in Jamestown Virginia (Colony established 1607)
Colorism	1619	Present	The discriminatory practice of treatment of a person being based on skin color; in addition to the divide and conquer strategy of treating black people with lighter skin tones more favorable than those of darker tones. Effects of which remain global today.
Massacres	1619	Present	Mass killings of black people either due to hate, jealousy or to put an end to economic success (wealth) black communities had achieved.
Slave Codes	1705	1865	Stripped all black people free or indentured of rights in order to control them.
Sundown Towns	1714	1964	Community of all white people which requires black people to either be out by sundown or not visit at all.
States Rights	1775	1783	The argument that state law can supersede federal or national law mostly pertains to maintaining slavery against federal regulation.
Fugitive Slave Clause	1787	1787	Preventing escaped slaves from claiming freedom when escaping to a free state gave enslavers the right to claim slaves.
Three-Fifths Compromise	1789	1789	3/5 of the total number of black people = to one person (Northern abolitionists' way of limiting southern representation in Congress).
Importation Ban	1808	1808	Congress bans the importation of slaves (hostages).
Black Literacy Ban	1820	1839	Prevented black people from learning how to read or write.
Missouri Compromise	1820	1857	Allowed union statehood while maintaining a balance between slave states and free states.
Race Riots	1829	Present	Riots that occur over racial tensions between black and white people. Oftentimes results in the loss of life of black people.
Manifest Destiny	1845	1865	A belief to force natives off the land and expand slavery to build the nation.
Convict Leasing	1846	1933	Government leasing of inmates to keep the southern economy moving with a nearly free labor force. Leased to railways, mines, and plantations and were subject to inhumane conditions.
Industrial Slavery	1850	1850	Bibb Steam Mill Company Corporations began owning slaves in addition to rich plantation owners.
Fugitive Slave Act	1850	1861	Forced abolitionists to turn in escaped slaves or be prosecuted to extent of the law.
Dred Scott Supreme Court Decision	1857	1857	Black people had no rights, were considered inferior, and were not included as citizens mentioned in the constitution.
Eugenics	1859	1945	Ideal to keep white people dominant through genetics as a way to advance the population.
Cornerstone speech	1861	1861	Alexander H. Stevens VP of the Confederacy stated that black people should be subservient to white people in the new government and confederate states will succeed from the Union because of it.
Southern Secession	1861	1865	In order to preserve slavery southern states succeed from the union.
Sequestration Act of 1861	1861	1861	Factories owned by Northerners were confiscated by southerners and utilized slave labor.
Confiscation act of 1861	1861	1861	Northern act of classifying escaped southern slaves as contraband of war; still viewed slaves as property, not people.
Civil War	1861	1865	American war over slavery.
Abraham Lincoln's Letter to Horace Greeley	1862	1862	President admits that his goal was solely to keep the union together whatever result of slavery he chooses would have to be the best option for the union.
Emancipation Proclamation	1863	1863	Allowed the Union army to enlist black men to fight in the war in an effort to change the way black people were viewed.
Confederate Government	1863	1865	Purchased Briar Field Ironworks in Alabama utilized slave labor (black men listed as livestock).
Special Field Order 15	1865	1865	Divided up 400 thousand acres amongst freedmen with 40 acres and a mule to each family.
Freedman Bureau	1865	1865	Protect the rights of freed slaves and assist with the distribution of 40 acres of land.
Lincoln Assassination	1865	1865	President Lincoln was killed resulting in known racist becoming president.
Andrew Johnson new President	1865	1869	The belief of country & government for white men only (Letter to Missouri Governor 1866).
KKK	1865	1872	American terrorist organization.
Reconstruction	1865	1877	Federal Troops protected rights for newly freed slaves allowing black males equality and voting rights.
Labor Contracts	1865	1964	Black people were forced into slave conditions through contracts.
Segregation	1865	1964	The systematic separation of people into racial or other ethnic groups in daily life.
Freedman Bureau	1866	1866	By order of President Andrew Johnson made freedmen (black people) return the land over to white ownership.
Civil Rights Act of 1866	1866	1866	All persons born in the United States are full-fledged citizens (Andrew Johnson vetoed congress override).
Reconstruction Act of 1867	1867	1867	Contained conditions for confederate states to comply with before joining back into the union. (Andrew Johnson's veto was overridden by Congress)
14th Amendment	1868	1868	Granted citizenship and equal civil and legal rights to black people and enslaved people who had been emancipated after the American Civil War. (Andrew Johnson denounced and referred to as States' Rights' was overridden by Congress)
Federal Gov Declaration of KKK	1870	1870	Deemed terrorist organization by federal government disbanded by 1872.
Compromise of 1877	1877	1877	Southern Democrats under President Rutherford B. Hayes pulled federal troops from the south. Eliminating protections for newly freed black people and undoing the Reconstruction period.
Neo Slavery (2nd Slavery)	1877	1941	The new form of slavery after chattel slavery was abolished consisted of debt peonage, industrial slavery & convict leasing. Often more cruel practices than plantation slavery because it did not require the preservation of slaves.
Debt Peonage	1877	1941	Slavery contract black people had to adhere to until the debt was paid off with labor usually keeping them in debt by false billings of food and lodging.
Black Codes	1877	1964	Vagrancy, trespassing, drinking, gambling, riding the train without a ticket, and obscene language were the petty crimes that got black people arrested and sentenced to hard labor.
Pig Laws	1877	1964	Was the process of elevating petty crimes to felonies for black people to force them into industrial slavery.
Confessing Judgement	1877	Present	Black people falsely accept judgment in order to avoid more harsh sentencing by trial.
Lynching	1877	Present	The murder of black people without trial or jury.
Policing	1877	Present	Unfair harassment, arrest, and killings of black people.
Civil Rights Cases Supreme Court	1883	1883	The Civil Rights Act of 1875 was reversed by the supreme court.
Homer Plessy Supreme Court	1896	1896	Federal Approval of Segregation 1/8 black Plessy was arrested in 1892 for failure to remove from the whites-only railcar.
Brown paper Bag Test	1900	1959	Due to the effects of colorism, many lighter-toned black people began throwing exclusive events where admittance was based on skin tone being lighter than a brown paper bag.
Disenfranchisement	1901	1965	Deprived black people of the right to vote usually through literacy tests, poll taxes, or intimidation. Caused no black jurors or black people to reside in government.
Birth Of a Nation	1915	1915	Originally called the Clansman a film that depicted black people as unintelligent and immoral.
President Woodrow Wilson	1915	1915	Viewed Birth of a Nation film in the White House.
Rebirth of the KKK	1915	Present	Ku Klux Klan Americas white supremacist, a terrorist hate group.
Tuskeegee Experiment	1932	1972	The largest known illegal medical experimentation on black people resulted in purposefully infecting black people with syphilis.
Redlining	1933	1988	Government-sponsored housing segregation plan to curb housing shortage by providing housing to white people while pushing black people to projects. Loans were usually approved for white areas and denied for black and mixed races. Also responsible for creating an even larger wealth gap between black and white people.
Green Book	1936	1967	Hugo Victor Green created a guidebook for black people that included restaurants, hotels, gas & drug stores that were necessary for safe travel. Black people would otherwise be turned away, humiliated, or harmed for seeking service while traveling within parts of the country.

Event	Start	End	Description
Circular 3591	1941	1941	Mandated FBI rebrand cases of peonage to involuntary servitude or slavery and prosecute as crimes.
Alfred Irving	1942	1942	Last chattel slave known to be freed in America.
Cointel Pro	1956	1971	Illegal projects conducted by the United States Federal Bureau of Investigation (FBI) aimed at surveilling, infiltrating, discrediting, and disrupting domestic American political organizations. Primarily black leaders and black organizations were often harassed, infiltrated & dismantled.
Civil Rights Act 1964	1964	1964	Prohibits discrimination based on race, color, religion, sex, or national origin
Voting Rights Act 1965	1965	1965	Ends discriminatory voting practices (disenfranchisement).
Mass Incarceration	1970	Present	Disproportionate incarceration of black people.
War on Drugs	1971	Present	Nixon's policy disenfranchised black people intentionally by imprisonment.
Three Strike Law	1994	Present	Law that allowed for longer sentencing with multiple offenses. Oftentimes black people would be convicted of multiple petty crimes that under 3 strikes law would allow them to be sentenced longer without a chance of probation.
Crime Bill 1994	1994	Present	Law proposed by Joe Biden and signed by Bill Clinton incentivized state and local government through federal funding (taxpayer dollars) to build more prisons, arrest more people and enact harsher sentencing that disproportionately affects African Americans.
FBI Black Identity Extremist Classification	2017	2017	FBI classifies Black Identity Extremists (BIEs) as the highest terror threat more so than any other group. Unwarranted BIE classification was so broad that you can literally classify any African American as BIE.
74 Million Americans	2020	2020	74 million people voted for President Trump after evident ties of supporting white nationalism that often coincides with white supremacy.
Restrictions of teaching Black History	2021	Present	Republican Governors pass restrictive laws about teaching black history in schools.
Voting Law Restrictions	2021	Present	Republican Governors pass restrictive laws to limit voting for certain groups
Supreme Court Decision	2022	Present	Supreme court guts wrongful conviction lifeline in favor of racist troupe 'States rights' which will largely affect innocent black people from being released from wrongful state convictions.

Create your list of historical events.

Event	Start Date	End Date	Summary

Look up the date of birth for the President of the United States, State Senators, Congress Representatives & Supreme Court Justices. Compare each date to the timeline and see what negative events they have lived through in their lifetime. Check and see if they have ever created, signed, or voted on policies or laws to eliminate or continue the disparities that occurred during the events listed.

Reparations *(rep·uhr·rAY·shuhnz)- the making of amends for a wrong one has done, by paying money to or otherwise helping those who have been wronged.*

My Reparations Ideas

Reparations
400 years of free college/vocational school tuition
400 years of federal and state tax exemption
400 years of 0% interest on mortgage loans
Free extensive genealogy DNA testing
Free healthcare
Rewrite all US History books with the inclusion of minority-based history professionals.
Mandatory lie detection testing for all doctors, law enforcement, lawyers, judges, and government personnel. To weed out bias, prejudice, dislike, and hate. No tolerance plan for discrimination to work in any listed industry.
100% voter and election transparency (all votes published and known to the public)
An official outlined US apology for all known atrocities towards minorities from slavery to all discriminatory practices up to the present day.
Redo any national symbol or anthem constructed before minorities had equal rights. (US flag / national anthem / etc)

List your reparations ideas

Reparations

Please check out my first book

Scan the QR code below to purchase the book.

Thank you!

Available for a limited time only, download book resources by scanning the QR code below.

www.ingramcontent.com/pod-product-compliance
Lightning Source LLC
Chambersburg PA
CBHW040727060526
44119CB00084B/350